D0460741

NIGHTMARE PLAGUES

MALARIA
Super Killer!

by Stephen Person

Consultant: Sean T. Prigge
Associate Professor
Johns Hopkins Bloomberg School of Public Health

BEARPORT
PUBLISHING

New York, New York

Credits

Cover and Title Page, © Parthajig Datta/AFP/Newscom; 4, © Thomas Cockrem/Alamy; 5, © Dawn Dubsky via Chicago Tribune/MCT/Newscom; 6L, © Antonio Perez/Chicago Tribune/MCT/Newscom; 6R, © Antonio Perez/ Chicago Tribune/MCT/Newscom; 7, © Antonio Perez/Chicago Tribune/MCT/Newscom; 9, © Crispin Hughes/ Hutchison Archive/Eye Ubiquitous/Alamy; 10, Courtesy of The Centers for Disease Control and Prevention; 11T, © Ulrich Doering/Alamy; 11B, Nicholas Bergkessel, Jr./Photo Researchers, Inc.; 12L, © Parthajig Datta/AFP/Newscom; 12R, © David Mack/Photo Researchers, Inc.; 13, © AP Images/David Longstreath; 14, © The Art Archive/Musée d'Orsay Paris/Dagli Orti/SuperStock; 15T, © Krystyna Szulecka/Alamy; 15B, © O. Diez/ArcoImages/Peter Arnold, Inc.; 16, © SuperStock; 17, © John Thomson/Hulton Archive/Getty Images; 18L, © Mary Evans Picture Library/ Alamy; 18R, © W. Beloi/Henry Guttmann/Hulton Archive/Getty Images; 19T, © Topical Press Agency/Hulton Archive/ Getty Images; 19B, © Margaret Aguirre/International Medical Corps/Reuters/Landov; 20, © Bettmann/Corbis; 21, © Bettmann/Corbis; 22, © Beawiharta/Reuters/Landov; 23, © Andy Crump/TDR/World Health Organization/Photo Researchers, Inc.; 24, © AP Images/David Longstreath; 25, © John-Michael Maas/Darby Communications; 26, © AP Images/Yves Logghe; 27, Courtesy of the World Bank/Suprotik Basu; 28, © Mary Evans Picture Library; 29, © Des Willie/Comic Relief/Getty Images; 31, Courtesy of The Centers for Disease Control and Prevention.

Publisher: Kenn Goin
Senior Editor: Lisa Wiseman
Creative Director: Spencer Brinker
Design: Dawn Beard Creative
Photo Researcher: Picture Perfect Professionals, LLC

Library of Congress Cataloging-in-Publication Data

Person, Stephen.
  Malaria : super killer! / by Stephen Person.
      p. cm. — (Nightmare plagues)
  Includes bibliographical references and index.
  ISBN-13: 978-1-936088-07-2 (library binding)
  ISBN-10: 1-936088-07-X (library binding)
  1. Malaria—Juvenile literature. I. Title.
  RC157.P47 2011
  614.5'32—dc22

                                    2010012018

For more information, write to Bearport Publishing Company, Inc., 101 Fifth Avenue, Suite 6R, New York, New York 10003. Printed in the United States of America in North Mankato, Minnesota.

072010
042110CGD

10 9 8 7 6 5 4 3 2 1

Contents

A Dangerous Decision

In February 2008, Dawn Dubsky left her home in Chicago, Illinois, for a two-week vacation in Ghana. Dawn was a nurse. She knew that **malaria** was a threat in the African country. Still, she decided not to take the medicine that could help protect her from the disease. She didn't want the possible **side effects**, such as stomach cramps, to ruin her trip. Unfortunately, the decision put her in terrible danger.

AFRICA

Ghana

Indian
Ocean

Atlantic
Ocean

N
W E
S

Ghana is a small country in West Africa.

Dawn loves to travel the world, and had always dreamed of seeing Africa. This photo shows an outdoor market in Ghana.

The day after returning to Chicago from her vacation, Dawn began to feel sick. Her head pounded and she felt extremely weak. That night she began shivering. A few hours later, she got a high fever that shot up to 103°F (39.4°C). Dawn knew what these **symptoms** meant. She rushed to the hospital.

Dawn walks across a bridge in Ghana's Kakum National Park. This photo was taken just days before she got sick.

There are about 1,500 cases of malaria each year in the United States. Nearly all the victims are travelers who **contracted** the disease in Africa or Asia, and brought it home.

A New Mission

Doctors did blood tests, and discovered that Dawn had malaria. They gave her drugs that usually cure the disease. Yet Dawn grew sicker. The disease caused so little blood to reach her arms and legs that her muscles slowly began to die. Unfortunately, doctors had to **amputate** all four of her limbs.

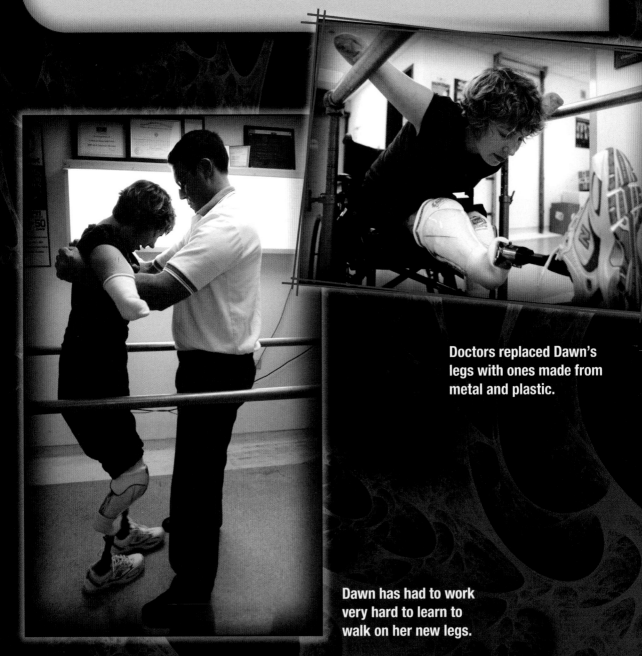

Doctors replaced Dawn's legs with ones made from metal and plastic.

Dawn has had to work very hard to learn to walk on her new legs.

After a few scary days, the medicine that doctors had given her finally started working. While Dawn recovered, she began learning about malaria. She found that it is one of the deadliest diseases in the world. "Luckily, my life was saved," she said, "but millions of children in Africa, their lives aren't saved." After her ordeal, Dawn decided to dedicate herself to the fight against malaria.

In 2009, Dawn founded America Against Malaria, a group that works to defeat malaria in Ghana and other malaria-stricken areas through education, prevention, and treatment.

When Dawn gives talks to try to raise money for her organization, she tells people, "By donating tonight, you're probably going to save a child's life in Africa."

Malaria Today

As Dawn learned, malaria was once common in most parts of the world. Today it has been wiped out in many areas, but it is still found in more than 100 countries, such as Peru in South America, Cambodia in Southeast Asia, and Uganda in Africa. About half the world's population lives in areas where malaria is common.

Malaria Around the World

Most cases of malaria occur in areas around the world that have very warm weather.

Dawn also discovered that there are 300 to 500 million cases of malaria in the world every year, with more than one million deaths. Sadly, most of the victims are children under the age of five living in **Sub-Saharan Africa**. It has been reported that every 30 seconds a child in Africa dies from this terrible disease.

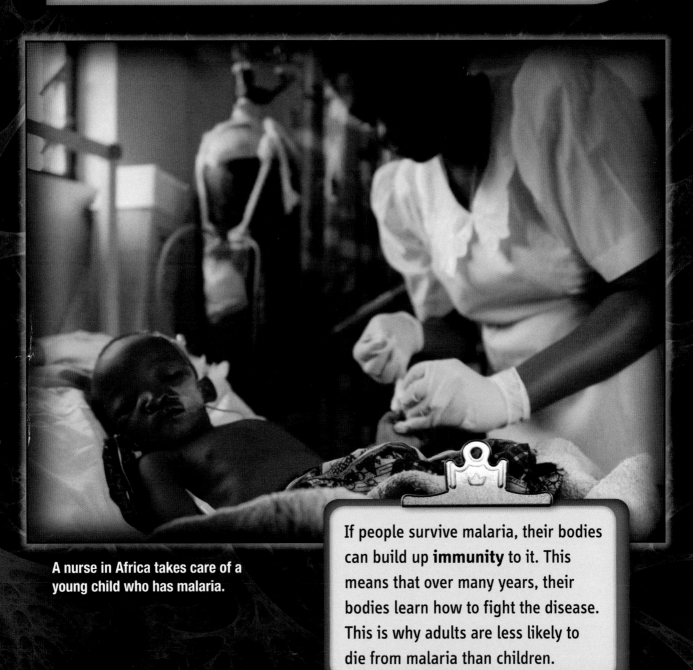

A nurse in Africa takes care of a young child who has malaria.

If people survive malaria, their bodies can build up **immunity** to it. This means that over many years, their bodies learn how to fight the disease. This is why adults are less likely to die from malaria than children.

Blood and Mosquitoes

Malaria is a disease spread from person to person only by female *Anopheles* (AH-no-fee-liz) mosquitoes. They need blood to produce their eggs, and often get it by biting people. When a person who has malaria is bitten, the mosquito sucks in the **parasites** that cause the disease along with the blood.

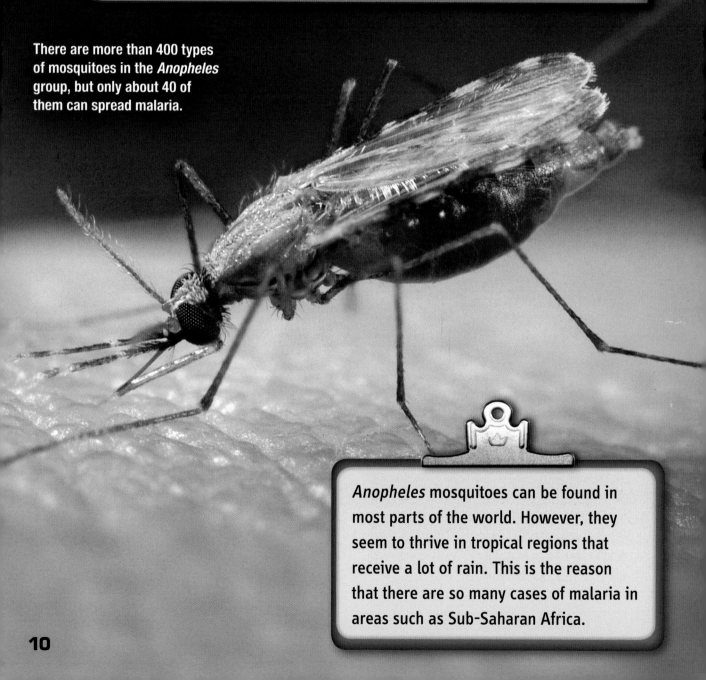

There are more than 400 types of mosquitoes in the *Anopheles* group, but only about 40 of them can spread malaria.

Anopheles mosquitoes can be found in most parts of the world. However, they seem to thrive in tropical regions that receive a lot of rain. This is the reason that there are so many cases of malaria in areas such as Sub-Saharan Africa.

The parasites live in the mosquito until it is ready to bite again. When the mosquito bites another person, the malaria parasites pass into that person's blood. From there, the parasites travel to the **liver**, where they multiply. At first, victims have no idea they are sick. That changes very quickly, however.

Mosquitoes like to lay their eggs in warm, standing water, like this puddle-filled street in Mozambique, a country in Africa.

Mosquitoes do not just spread malaria to humans. They can also spread it to animals such as flying squirrels (shown here), birds, mice, monkeys, snakes, and bats.

Chills, Fever, and Death

Malaria victims usually begin to feel sick one to two weeks after being bitten. That's when thousands of parasites leave the victim's liver and travel through his or her bloodstream, attacking and destroying **red blood cells**.

At first, a malaria victim feels tired and suffers head and muscle aches. Next, chills set in, and the person may shiver violently. The victim's temperature then rises suddenly, often up to 105°F (40.6°C). The sick person is soon covered in sweat.

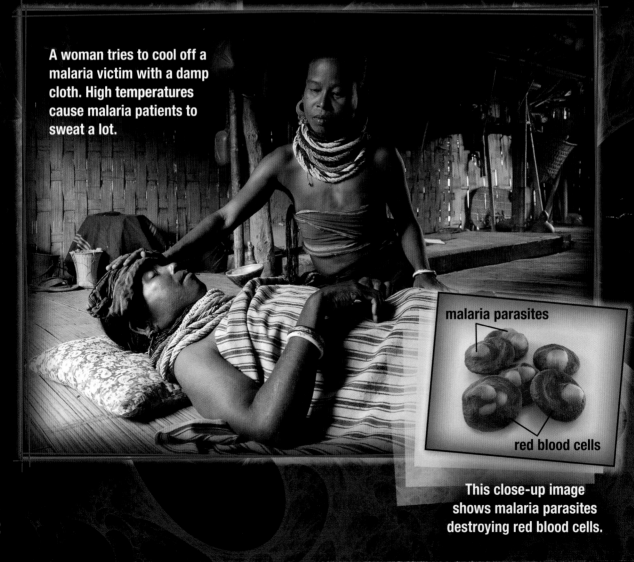

A woman tries to cool off a malaria victim with a damp cloth. High temperatures cause malaria patients to sweat a lot.

malaria parasites

red blood cells

This close-up image shows malaria parasites destroying red blood cells.

After several hours, the symptoms often disappear. Without treatment, however, the victim will start to feel sick all over again within a day or two. In the worst cases, a person's **vital organs** fail in just a few days, leading first to a **coma** and then to death.

Malaria's early symptoms are similar to those of other diseases such as the flu. Doctors determine if a person has malaria by looking at the patient's blood under a microscope and checking for malaria parasites.

A malaria researcher preparing blood samples

History of a Killer

Scientists believe malaria has existed for millions of years. Long ago, people did not know what caused the disease or how to cure it. Most people believed that a victim became sick with malaria by breathing in the smelly gases rising from swamps and marshes. In fact, the word malaria comes from the Italian term *mal aria*, meaning "bad air."

Malaria victims in Italy

A turning point in the fight against the disease came in the early 1600s. At that time, many **missionaries** from Spain were working in South America. They noticed something amazing. Native people of the Andes Mountains knew how to treat malaria. To do so, they pounded the bark from cinchona (sin-KOH-na) trees into powder. Then they mixed the powder into water and drank it. The Spanish tried this treatment themselves. Sure enough, it not only stopped the malaria symptoms, but it cured them of the disease.

In the 1600s, cinchona trees, shown here, became known as "fever trees" because of their ability to cure fevers caused by malaria.

Scientists later discovered the ingredient in cinchona bark that fights malaria. They named it quinine, and it's still used to treat malaria today.

cinchona bark

Stealing the Cure

Once cinchona bark became known as a cure for malaria, it became very valuable. European countries wanted to plant cinchona trees in their own **colonies** in Asia. To do this, they would have to take some of the cinchona plants out of South America and bring them to Asia. South American governments, however, wanted to have control of the valuable cinchona bark. They refused to let people from other nations take the live trees out of their countries.

Today, some people still use cinchona bark to treat malaria. Here, a woman strips bark from cinchona tree branches.

In the 1800s, Britain was in desperate need of a cheap quinine source. One reason was that in the British colony of India, nearly two million people were dying of malaria each year. Having their own cinchona **plantations** could help solve this problem.

In the 1860s, British scientists decided to steal some of the trees. They hacked their way into the rain forest and secretly dug up the live plants. They packed them into crates, and carried them by mule over the Andes Mountains to the coast of the Pacific Ocean. Then the plants were loaded onto ships that left for Asia.

Cinchona plants need to be kept warm or they will not survive. While crossing the freezing Andes with fragile cinchona plants, scientist Clements Markham slept with some of the plants in his arms to keep them from dying of cold.

Cinchona trees are native to the rain forests of the Andes Mountains in South America. They grow best in warm, wet climates.

Science Breaks Through

The stolen cinchona trees were planted in India and other warm parts of Asia. Seeds from the stolen trees were also collected so that more trees could be planted. As a result, quinine became cheap and widely available by the late 1800s.

Though doctors had a treatment for the disease, they still didn't understand its cause. Then, in 1880, a French doctor named Alphonse Laveran made a major discovery. While studying the blood of malaria victims under a microscope, he found the parasites that cause the disease.

Alphonse Laveran received the Nobel Prize for Medicine in 1907. Each year, this prize is awarded to a scientist who makes important medical discoveries.

This photo shows British government officials standing in front of a newly planted cinchona tree plantation.

Then, in 1897, a British officer named Ronald Ross figured out how the disease spreads. While **dissecting** mosquitoes that had bitten malaria victims, he discovered malaria parasites inside their stomachs. He realized that the mosquitoes spread these parasites by biting people.

Ronald Ross in his office at the Ross Institute and Hospital for Tropical Diseases

In the 1930s and 1940s, scientists began developing new drugs to treat malaria. Like quinine, they attack the malaria parasites in victims' blood. These new drugs are cheaper than quinine, and easier to make in very large quantities.

This child in Africa is getting treatment for malaria. Today, modern medicines can usually cure people of this deadly disease.

Starting to Win the Fight

The discoveries of what causes malaria and how it spreads quickly changed history. In 1904, the United States began building a **canal** across Panama in Central America. This was considered a very risky project. Why? The French had tried to build a canal there in the 1880s. More than 20,000 workers died from malaria and **yellow fever**, and the project was abandoned.

Workers building the Panama Canal

Before the canal was built, ships traveling from one coast of the United States to the other had to sail around South America. By traveling through the canal instead, these trips were about 9,000 miles (14,484 km) shorter.

NORTH AMERICA

Atlantic Ocean

Panama Canal

PANAMA

Pacific Ocean

SOUTH AMERICA

N W E S

The Americans faced a similar problem until an officer named William Gorgas came up with a plan to attack disease-carrying mosquitoes. He drained pools of water where mosquitoes **bred**. He also put up screens to keep mosquitoes out of the buildings where workers slept. These safety measures helped save the lives of many people. Only about half as many people died as when the French were trying to build the canal. The Panama Canal was finally completed by 1914.

Gorgas, shown here, helped show the world how to attack malaria.

Malaria was a serious problem in the warm and wet southeastern United States in the early 1900s. To control the disease, workers drained swampy areas where mosquitoes bred, and sprayed **insecticides** to kill the insects. By 1951, malaria was wiped out in the United States.

The Battle Continues

In 1955, the **World Health Organization** (WHO) led an effort to wipe out malaria across the globe. New insecticides were used to kill mosquitoes in areas with malaria. The disease was wiped out in Europe and Australia by 1969. Malaria cases also dropped sharply in India.

Spraying areas with insecticide to kill mosquitoes helps stop the spread of malaria.

Unfortunately, WHO failed to reach its goal of destroying malaria in Sub-Saharan Africa. Why? This area is the poorest part of the world. Many countries don't have enough money to buy malaria medicines or the tools they need to keep mosquitoes away. For example, an effective way for people to protect themselves from contracting malaria is to sleep under mosquito nets that have been soaked in insecticide. The nets cost about $10 each. Yet even that is too expensive for many families.

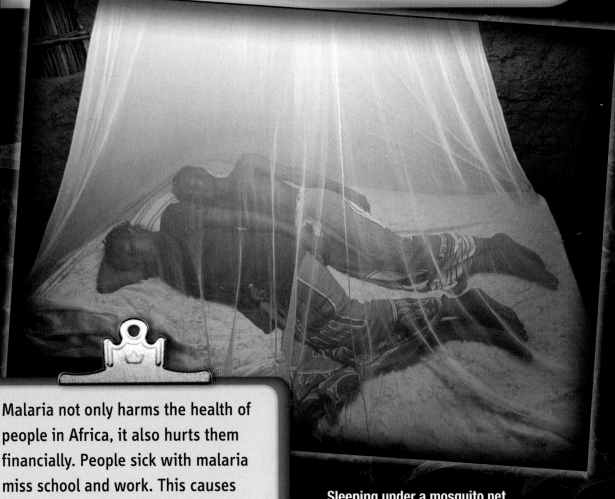

Malaria not only harms the health of people in Africa, it also hurts them financially. People sick with malaria miss school and work. This causes them to earn less money—making countries with malaria poorer than those without the disease.

Sleeping under a mosquito net protects people from getting bitten by mosquitoes, which usually feed at night.

New Fear, New Hope

Though medicines today can cure most cases of malaria, some of the parasites that cause the disease have changed and become **resistant** to malaria medicines. That's why scientists must keep making new medicines to fight the disease.

This health worker brings malaria medicine to villages in Cambodia, in Southeast Asia. Malaria parasites in this region have become resistant to some malaria drugs.

One possible solution to the problem of malaria's drug resistance is a malaria **vaccine**. This treatment would allow a person to build up immunity to malaria before being exposed to the parasites. Currently, several teams of scientists are working on malaria vaccines. One vaccine is already being tested on 5,000 children in Africa. If it works, it may be available to more people by 2012. "This is a tremendous moment in the fight against malaria," says Dr. Joe Cohen, one of the vaccine's creators.

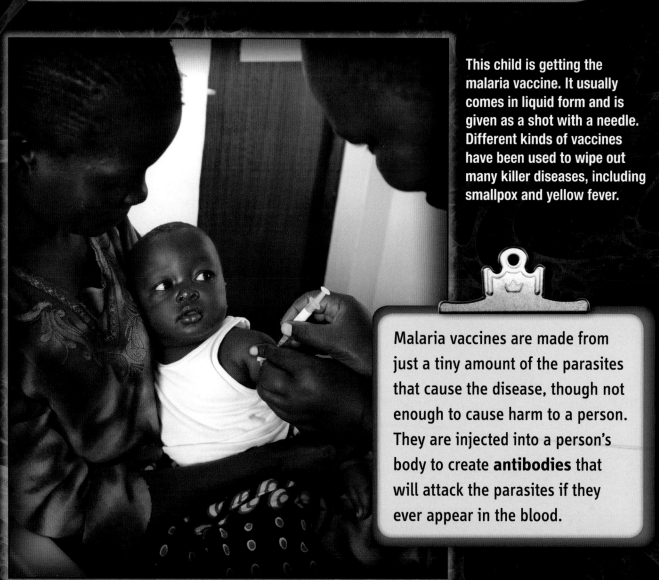

This child is getting the malaria vaccine. It usually comes in liquid form and is given as a shot with a needle. Different kinds of vaccines have been used to wipe out many killer diseases, including smallpox and yellow fever.

Malaria vaccines are made from just a tiny amount of the parasites that cause the disease, though not enough to cause harm to a person. They are injected into a person's body to create **antibodies** that will attack the parasites if they ever appear in the blood.

United Against Malaria

Charles Ssali (SAH-lee) is not waiting for a vaccine. This 12-year-old soccer lover from Uganda, in Africa, survived malaria when he was a young boy. He knows how terrible the disease is. Now Charles travels around the world for the United Against Malaria program. He helps educate people about treatments for the disease. "I hope my global journey will help soccer fans all over the world understand this disease," he says.

Charles asks world leaders to sign his soccer ball in support of the fight against malaria. "I can bring it back to our African leaders," he says, "and show them how the world is behind us in our efforts to end malaria."

Many international organizations—such as The Global Fund to Fight AIDS, Tuberculosis and Malaria—are working to fight malaria. Since 2002, this group has given away more than 100 million mosquito nets and more than 100 million malaria drug treatments to people living in countries with the disease.

As Charles tells people, malaria *can* be defeated. With enough insecticides, medicines, and mosquito nets, the world can wipe out this super killer.

April 25 has been named World Malaria Day. Around the world, people participate in events to raise awareness of the fight against this terrible killer. These schoolchildren are celebrating the day by displaying a sign they made.

Famous Malaria Outbreaks

Malaria parasites have existed for millions of years. Some scientists believe malaria has killed more people than any other disease in human history. Here's information about famous malaria **outbreaks** of the past.

Rome, Italy (1623)

- Malaria swept through Rome, Italy, in 1623, killing Pope Gregory XV (15) and many other people.

- Leaders of the Catholic Church then met to select a new pope. Dozens of church officials died during the meetings, as mosquitoes spread malaria among them.

- It was soon after this outbreak that people in Italy first heard about the cinchona tree. There was a huge demand for the bark—but it was hard to get, and expensive, because South American governments had strict control over it.

U.S. Civil War (1861–1865)

- Unlike soldiers from the South, soldiers from the North came from areas without malaria. They had no immunity to the disease. So while fighting in the South, these soldiers faced the disease for the first time.

- The Northern Army had 1.3 million cases of malaria. More than 10,000 soldiers died from the illness.

World War I (1914–1918)

- Soldiers fighting in a part of southern Europe called Macedonia contracted malaria in huge numbers. Eighty percent of France's 120,000 soldiers fighting in this area were hospitalized with the disease. When ordered to attack the enemy, a French general said, "Regret that my army is in the hospital with malaria."

- From 1916 to 1918, about 23,000 British soldiers were killed or wounded in the fight for Macedonia, while more than 160,000 suffered from malaria.

- Thousands of sick British soldiers were sent home to recover. Unfortunately, they brought the malaria parasites with them, causing new outbreaks in British cities.

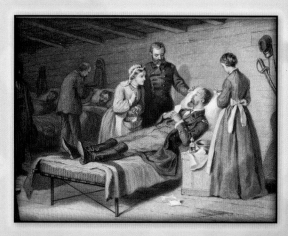

A U.S. Civil War soldier infected with malaria

Malaria Facts

There are five different forms of the malaria parasite that infect people. All forms cause severe illness, but only one, *Plasmodium falciparum*, is usually deadly if not treated quickly. Here are some more facts about malaria.

Malaria Prevention

- In areas where malaria is common, people should do everything possible to avoid being bitten by mosquitoes. This includes using insect repellent and sleeping under mosquito nets treated with insecticide.

- It is also important to eliminate breeding places for mosquitoes by draining areas of standing water, especially near houses.

- Mosquitoes can also be killed with insecticide spray.

What to Do

- If traveling to an area with malaria, people should begin taking malaria medicine before leaving home in order to prevent getting the disease.

- Anyone who thinks he or she may have malaria should see a doctor right away. A blood test will show if malaria parasites are in a person's blood.

- Malaria victims must begin taking malaria medication right away, before the disease becomes life threatening.

Tracking Malaria Today

- WHO works with countries around the world to track malaria cases.

- The group's experts help provide poor countries with the tools they need to treat new cases of malaria.

Many organizations help fight malaria by giving out mosquito nets.

Glossary

amputate (AM-pyoo-*tayt*) to remove a part of the body, often an arm or leg; usually done when a body part is diseased or too badly wounded to be saved

antibodies (AN-ti-bod-eez) substances in the blood that help fight disease

bred (BRED) had young

canal (kuh-NAL) a path made to connect bodies of water so that boats can travel between them

colonies (KOL-uh-neez) areas that have been settled by people from another country and are ruled by that country

coma (KOH-muh) a state in which a person is unconscious and cannot wake up; can be caused by disease

contracted (kon-TRAKT-id) got a disease

dissecting (dye-SEKT-ing) cutting something open in order to examine it

immunity (i-MYOO-ni-tee) the ability to resist a disease

insecticides (in-SEK-tuh-sides) poisons used to kill insects

liver (LIV-ur) a large important organ in the human body that cleans the blood

malaria (muh-LAIR-ee-uh) a disease transmitted to humans by the bite of female *Anopheles* mosquitoes, causing chills, fever, sweating, and even death

missionaries (MISH-uh-*nair*-eez) people sent, often to another country, to teach; often sent by religious groups

outbreaks (OUT-*brakes*) occasions when a number of cases of a disease suddenly appear at the same time

parasites (PA-ruh-*sites*) living creatures that get food by living on or in another plant or animal

plantations (plan-TAY-shuhnz) large farms where crops or trees are grown

red blood cells (RED BLUHD SELZ) cells in a person's blood that carry oxygen to every part of the body

resistant (ri-ZISS-tuhnt) immune to; not affected by medicine

side effects (SIDE uh-FEKTS) unwanted or unintended effects of a medicine

Sub-Saharan Africa (*suhb*-suh-HAIR-in AF-ri-kuh) a region of Africa south of the Sahara Desert

symptoms (SIMP-tuhmz) signs of a disease felt by a person; often feelings of pain or discomfort

vaccine (vak-SEEN) medicine that protects people against a disease

vital organs (VYE-tuhl OR-guhnz) parts of the body, such as the brain, lungs, and liver, that are needed to keep a person alive

World Health Organization (WURLD HELTH *or*-guh-nuh-ZAY-shuhn) a group of doctors, scientists, and other health workers that monitors disease outbreaks and works to improve the health of people around the world

yellow fever (YEL-oh FEE-vur) a disease spread by mosquitoes; it causes fever, aches, yellowing of skin, bleeding, and often death

Bibliography

Honigsbaum, Mark. *The Fever Trail: In Search of the Cure for Malaria.* New York: Farrar, Straus and Giroux (2001).

Packard, Randall. *The Making of a Tropical Disease: A Short History of Malaria.* Baltimore, MD: Johns Hopkins University Press (2007).

www.cdc.gov/malaria/about/index.html

Read More

Day, Nancy. *Malaria, West Nile, and Other Mosquito-Borne Diseases.* Berkeley Heights, NJ: Enslow Publishers (2001).

Isle, Mick. *Malaria.* New York: Rosen Publishing Group (2001).

Wyborny, Sheila. *The Malaria Parasite.* San Diego, CA: KidHaven Press (2005).

Learn More Online

To learn more about malaria, visit
www.bearportpublishing.com/NightmarePlagues

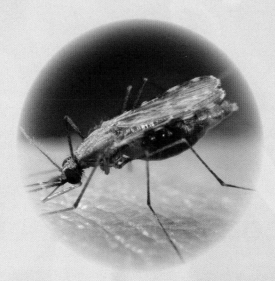

Index

About the Author

Stephen Person has written many children's books about
history, science, and the environment. He lives with his
family in Brooklyn, New York.